Vagrant

From newbie to professional in One Day!

By Sean Dunne

Table of Contents

Disclaimer

While all attempts have been made to verify the information provided in this book, the author does assume any responsibility for errors, omissions, or contrary interpretations of the subject matter contained within. The information provided in this book is for educational and entertainment purposes only. The reader is responsible for his or her own actions and the author does not accept any responsibilities for any liabilities or damages, real or perceived, resulting from the use of this information.

The trademarks that are used are without any consent, and the publication of the trademark is without permission or backing by the trademark owner. All trademarks and brands within this book are for clarifying purposes only and are the owned by the owners themselves, not affiliated with this document.

Introduction

Vagrant is a very important tool. After its initial release, it only supported integration with VirtualBox. However, currently, this tool can be used together with other tools such as VMWare and KVM. The tool is also used together with Docker, which is a good tool and can be used as an alternative for a complete operating system. This book explores the Vagrant tool, and how you can use to accomplish your tasks. Enjoy reading!

Chapter 1- Vagrant Push

With Vagrant version 1.7 and above, we are able to push or deploy an application code in a similar directory as the Vagrant file to a remote location such as an FTP server.

The pushes have to be defined in the Vagrant file of your application and for us to invoke them; we use the subcommand *"vagrant push."* Just like the other Vagrant components, all Vagrant Push plugins have a very unique configuration. It is good for you to view your documentation and see the configuration of your Vagrant push. Consider the following code, which shows a section of Vagrant Push Configuration in the vagrantfile:

```
config.push.define "ftp" do |push|
 push.host = "ftp.company.com"
 push.username = "..."
```

```
  # ...
end
```

Once you are ready to deploy your app to the FTP server, just run the single command given below:

$ vagrant push

Just like providers in Vagrant providers, the Push also has many backend declarations which it supports. Consider the environment given below:

```
config.push.define "staging", strategy: "ftp" do |push|
  # ...
end

config.push.define "qa", strategy: "ftp" do |push|
```

```
  # ...
```

end

In such a case, the user will be expected to pass the Vagrant Push name to our subcommand as shown below:

$ vagrant push staging

The Vagrant Push provides us with the easiest way to deploy our applications.

FTP & SFTP Strategy

Vagrant Push SFTP and FTP strategy will push the code into the Vagrant development environment to a remote SFTP or FTP server. In this case, the following configuration options are supported:

- host- this is the address of our remote server, which is either FTP or SFTP. In case the server is being executed on a non-standard port. In such a case, the port can be specified after the address.

- username- this is the username which is to be used for the purpose of authentication with our server, either FTP or SFTP.

- password- this is the password which is to be used for the purpose of authentication with our server, either FTP or SFTP.

- passive- this uses passive FTP

- secure- this uses the secure SFTP

- destination- this represents the root destination on our target system for syncing the files. The default one is "/."

- exclude- this is used for adding a file pattern or a file for the purpose of excluding it from upload, and this is done relative to *"dir."* Specification of the value can be done multiple times, and this will become additive.

- dir- this is the base directory having the files which are to be uploaded. In most cases, this is set by default to vangrantfile, but for those with a *"bin"* or *"src"* folder, or maybe any other folder which you need to specify, you can change this from the default.

The Vagrant Push SFTP and FTP is defined in the file vagrantfile by use of the key *ftp*. This is shown below:

config.push.define "ftp" do |push|

 push.host = "ftp.company_name.com"

 push.username = "username"

 push.password = "password"

end

The application can then be pushed to the server, either SFTP or FTP:

$ vagrant push

Heroku Strategy

This is just a public PAAS strategy which makes it easy for us to deploy an application. With a Vagrant Push Heroku strategy, the code for the application is pushed to the Heroku. However, before you can be in a position to do this, you must have already configured the credentials of Heroku and then created your Heroku application.

In this tutorial, we will only push the files which have been committed to the Git repository will be pushed to the Heroku. Also, you have to note that the branch which is currently in use will have to be pushed to the Heroku even if it is not the master branch.

The following configuration options are supported in the Vagrant Push Heroku configuration:

1. app- this is the name of your Heroku application. If there is no Heroku app with such a name, then an exception will be raised. In case you do not specify a name for this parameter, then the basename of your directory which has your Vagrant file will be used as the name of the app. It is good for you to add the app setting to your Vagrant file, since this can be changed between the users.

2. dir- the base directory having the Git repository to be uploaded to the Heroku. By default, this represents the same directory as the Vagrant file, but in case you have already nested the Git directory, you can readily specify this.

3. remote- this is the name of your Git remote where you have configured your Heroku. The default value for this is "Heroku."

The *"heroku"* key has been used to define the Vagrant Push Heroku strategy in the Vagrant file. This is shown below:

```
config.push.define "heroku" do |push|
 push.app = "myapp"
end
```

The applicant can then be pushed to the Heroku using the following command:

```
$ vagrant push
```

Local Exec Strategy

With this type of strategy, a user is able to invoke a shell command which is arbitrary or a script which is part of the push. Note that with this strategy, no validation is done in terms of correctness, so you have to tackle this on your part.

The following configuration options are supported in this Vagrant Push strategy:

1. script- this is the path which leads to the script on the disk. In most cases, the vagrant will attempt to convert the script into an executable, but in case this fails, then an exception will be raised.

2. inline- this is the inline script which is to be executed.

3. args- these are the optional arguments which will be passed to the shell script during the process of

execution as a single string. You have to write these arguments as if they were directly typed on the command line, so ensure that you quote and escape characters as you are expected to do. The arguments can also be passed in an array and in such a case, the quoting will done on your behalf by the Vagrant.

Note that only one of the inline and script options will be specified in each single push notification.

The key "local-exec" has been used for definition of this strategy in the vagrantfile.

Remote path:

config.push.define "local-exec" do |push|

push.inline = <<-SCRIPT

```
scp -r . server:/var/www/website
SCRIPT
End
```

Local path:

```
config.push.define "local-exec" do |push|
push.inline = <<-SCRIPT
cp -r . /var/www/website
SCRIPT
end
```

For scripts which are more complicated, you may store them by use of a separate file, and then read from your vagrantfile and continue. This is shown below:

```
config.push.define "local-exec" do |push|
 push.script = "my-script.sh"
end
```

The push can then be invoked with Vagrant as shown below:

```
$ vagrant push
```

Atlas Strategy

This is just a commercial offering which provides us with a production environment for our Vagrant development environment. There are more notes online about the Atlas so you can read them. With this strategy, the code for our application will be pushed to the Atlas service of Hashicorp.

The strategy supports the following configuration options:

1. app- this is the name of the app in the Hashicop's Atlas. If the app doesn't exist, we will use a user confirmation so as to create it.

2. exclude- this is used for adding a file pattern or a file which should be excluded from the upload, and this is relative to your directory. The value for this can be

specified for several times, and it becomes additive. The *"exclude"* usually takes precedence over the values of *"include."*

3. include- this is used for adding a file pattern or a file which is to be included in the upload, and this is done relative to the directory. The value is additive, and we are free to specify as many times as we want.

4. dir- this is the base directory which has the files which are to be uploaded. The default setting is that this directory is similar to your Vagrant file. However, for those having a *"bin"* or *"src"* folder, this can be specified, or any other folder which may be in need of uploading.

5. vcs- if this has been set to true, then the Vagrant will automatically use the VCS data to determine the files which are to be uploaded. Any uncommitted changes will not be deployed at all.

Also, there are some additional options which are exposed for the power users of the Vagrant Atlas push strategy. However, these options are not used by most users. They include the following:

1. address- this is the address of the Atlas server to which the upload is to be done. The Public Atlas Server forms the default for this.

2. token- this represents the Atlas token which you are going to use. If you have run the command *"vagrant login,"* this will make use of the token which has been generated by the command. If you have set the "ATLAS_TOKEN" environment variable, this is the value which will be used by the uploader. By default, the value for this is set to nil.

The key *"atlas"* has been used for definition of Vagrant Push Atlas Strategy in the Vagrant file. This is shown below:

```
config.push.define "atlas" do |push|
 push.app = "username/application"
end
```

The following command can then be used for pushing the application to Atlas:

$ vagrant push

Chapter 2- Setting up LAMP in Vagrant

LAMP stands for Linux, Apache, MySQL, PHP. It is a web-development environment which is open-source and allows us to create web apps. For us to create this kind of web stack in Vagrant, the followings steps are necessary:

1. Create a directory in which the instance will be created. Use the commands given below:

   mkdir -p ~/Vagrant/lamp

   cd ~/Vagrant/lamp

2. It is now time for us to initialize the Vagrant box. There are two options on how to do this.

The first one is to reuse the Ubuntu 12.04 LTS box. The following command can be used for this purpose:

vagrant init precise32

Secondly, a fresh addition of the box can be done by downloading of the Ubuntu 12.04 LTS Vagrant box. Begin with the following command:

vagrant box add precise32
http://files.vagrantup.com /precise32.box

This should then be followed by the following command:

vagrant init precise32

3. It is now time for you to create the Vagrant file. The following command can be used for this purpose:

vagrant up

This can then be edited as shown below:

```
Vagrant.configure(2) do |config|
config.vm.box = "precise32"

# Mentioning the SSH Username/Password:
config.ssh.username = "vagrant"
config.ssh.password = "vagrant"
# Begin Configuring
config.vm.define "lamp" do|lamp|


lamp.vm.hostname = "lamp" # Setting up hostname
lamp.vm.network "private_network", ip:
"192.168.205.10" # Setting up machine's IP Address
lamp.vm.provision :shell, path: "script.sh" #
Provisioning with script.sh
end

# End Configuring
end
```

The commented lines have been deleted so that no confusion can be brought.

4.   At this point, we can begin to provision our LAMP installation. Create a shell script, and give it the name "*scipt.sh*" using your favorite text editor. The following should be the code for the file:

```bash
#!/bin/bash
# Updating the repository
sudo apt-get -y update
# Installing the Apache
sudo apt-get -y install apache2
# Installing MySQL together with its
dependencies, and setting up the root password
for the MySQL as it will prompt you to enter the
password during process of installation

sudo debconf-set-selections <<< 'mysql-server-
5.5 mysql-server/root_password password
rootpass'
sudo debconf-set-selections <<< 'mysql-server-
5.5 mysql-server/root_password_again
password rootpass'
sudo apt-get -y install mysql-server libapache2-
mod-auth-mysql php5-mysql


# Installing PHP and it's dependencies
sudo apt-get -y install php5 libapache2-mod-
php5 php5-mcrypt
```

5.   Once you have saved the script, execute the command

given below:

vagrant up

6.   Once the installation of Vagrant has completed, you can SSH into your Vagrant box. Use the following command:

vagrant ssh

7.   Use the following command to verify the installation:

dpkg -l | grep "apache2\|mysql-server-5.5\|php5"

All the packages should be listed, which should be an indication that the installation was done successfully. Once you are done with the above steps, you will have set up LAMP in Vagrant.

To save the box at its current state, follow the steps given below:

1. Get out of the Vagrant box by use of the command given below:

Exit

2.   Package the box using the command given below:

**vagrant package --output
ubuntu1204_LAMP.box**

The above command will create the file "ubuntu1204_LAMP.box" which one can use as a base box with the LAMP having already been installed. For you to stay very organized, you can create a directory in which all the boxes will be stored and then move the "ubuntu1204_LAMP.box" into it. Use the commands given below:

mkdir -p ~/Vagrant/boxes

mv ubuntu1204_LAMP.box ~/Vagrant/boxes

The box can be imported and initialized at any time as shown below:

vagrant init ubuntu1204_LAMP file:~/Vagrant/boxes/ubuntu1204_LAMP.box

Accessing the Database

Note that we do not have the phpMyAdmin at this point. This can easily be done via the provisioner, so opt for this if you need. A desktop client is better and most preferred by many users.

It is easy for us to establish a connection to the database in this example and we already have the credentials. For us to use PHP to establish the connection, we should use the credentials given below:

Host: localhost

User: **root**

Password: root

Port: 3306

If the connection is to be established via the sequel Pro, then the credentials should be as shown below:

MySQL Host: 172.22.22.22 (or the IP used)

User: root

Password: root

Port: 3306

Depending on the configuration of the Vagrant file, this type of connection might not succeed since you may be seen as if you are connecting from a remote location. The connection can also be done using a desktop client by employing the SSH forwarding trick.

MySQL Host: localhost or 127.0.0.1

User: root

Password: root

Port: 3306

SHH Host: 172.22.22.22

SSH User: vagrant

SSH Key: ~/.vagrant.d/insecure_private_key   (or your path to the private key)

Chapter 3- vagrant-omnibus

This is a Vagrant plugin which makes sure that the desired chef version has been installed by use of platform-specific Omnibus packages.

Installation

Begin by downloading and installing Vagrant version 1.1 and above. Install the tool by executing the following command:

$ vagrant plugin install vagrant-omnibus

Usage

The Omnibus plugin will automatically hook into Vagrant provisioning middleware. The config key "omnibus.chef_version" is used for the purpose of specifying the version of your Chef Omnibus package which you need to install. The latest version of Chef can be installed as shown below:

Vagrant.configure("2") do |config|

 config.omnibus.chef_version = :latest

 ...

End

To install a specific version of Chef, use the code given below:

Vagrant.configure("2") do |config|

 config.omnibus.chef_version = "11.4.0"

...

end

For specification of a custom install script, use the code given below:

```
Vagrant.configure("2") do |config|

 config.omnibus.install_url =
'http://acme.com/install.sh'

 # config.omnibus.install_url =
'http://acme.com/install.msi'

 # config.omnibus.install_url =
'/some/path/on/your/host'

 ...

end
```

The plugin is also multi vm ware, so installation of a different version on each machine will be possible. This is shown below:

```
Vagrant.configure("2") do |config|
 config.vm.define :new_chef do |new_chef_config|
  ...
  new_chef_config.omnibus.chef_version = :latest
  ...
 end
 config.vm.define :old_chef do |old_chef_config|
  ...
  old_chef_config.omnibus.chef_version = "10.24.0"
  ...
 end
end
```

Tests

Let us discuss the types of tests which we can perform.

Unit

This type of test can be carried out by execution of the command given below:

rake test:unit

Acceptance

This type of repository is currently shipped with an acceptance test, and a basic one can be used for:

- Provision of an instance of Vagrant.

- An attempt to perform installation of Chef by use of the plugin.

- Performing a basic chef-solo run which will make sure that the Chef has been installed.

In the case of the acceptance tests, they can be executed against a subset of your Vagrant providers which have been listed above. The command given below can be used for the purpose of running the acceptance tests:

rake test:acceptance:PROVIDER_NAME

You should note that all acceptance tests make use of provisioner-less coudimages and baseboxes.

Chapter 4- Vagrant Commands

You might be aware of the primary Vagrant commands. However, there are some extra commands which can be seen as being non-primary. Let us discuss these commands.

Docker commands

The Docker provider gives some other Vagrant commands which can be used for the purpose of interaction with Docker containers. This helps with the workflow on top of the Vagrant so that one can gain full access to the Docker.

docker logs

We can use the "vagrant docker-logs" for the purpose of viewing the logs of a currently running container. You have to note that most Docker containers are a single-process, and that is why they are used for the purpose of viewing the logs of that one particular process. It is also possible for us to tail the commands.

docker run

We can use the "vagrant docker-run" so as to run one-off commands against our Docker container. The Docker container which has been started will share the links, volumes, and others. Consider the example given below:

$ vagrant docker-run app -- rake db:migrate

The above command will run the "rake db:migrate" in the contest of our app container.

RSYNC

This command takes the syntax given below:

vagrant rsync

The command will force a resync of the rsync synced folders. Note that in case any change is made on these types of folders such as exclusion of the paths, one will have to execute the command *"vagrant reload"* so as to make the changes take effect.

rsync-auto

This command will watch all of the directories of the rsync synced folders and then initiate an automatic rsync transfer whenever changes have been detected. The command will not exit until one receives an interrupt.

The change detection has been optimized so that it can make use of APIs which are API specific, and listen for changes in the file system, and it will not just poll the directory.

The command takes the following syntax:

vagrant rsync-auto

The following option can be used in the command:

-- [no-]poll- this will force Vagrant to watch for changes by use of the file system polling rather than the file system events. This is normally required for file systems which are not in need of support events. However, it is good for you to note that once this has been enabled, the rsync-auto will be made much slower. The default setting is that polling has been disabled.

Machine State Changes

The command *"rsycn-auto"* will not currently handle any machine changes effectively. An example is when you have started the *"rsync-auto"* command and then stop your guest machine, and then perform some changes to your files and then boot it back; the *"rsync-auto"* command will not attempt to perform a resync.

To ensure that your command runs as expected, just start the *"srync-auto"* only once you notice that the machine is running, and then shut it down before any state of the machine has changed. The *"rsync"* command can always be used for forcing a rsync to take place.

Vagrantfile Changes

If the vagrantfile is changed or moved, the command *"rsycn-auto"* will have to be restarted. An example of this is when you have added synced folders to the vagrantfile, or when the directory having the vagrantfile has been moved, the command *"rsycn-auto"* may end up not detecting the changes which you have made or even start to behave in a strange way.

This is why it is recommended that you first switch off the *"rsync-auto"* command, make your changes, and then restart it.

Let us discuss some other commands commonly used in Vagrant.

Snapshot Command

This command is used with the syntax given below:

vagrant snapshot

The command is used for the purpose of management of snapshots with your guest machine. Snapshots are used for recording a point-in-time state of a particular guest machine. Restoration can then be done to this environment. With this, you will be in a position to experiment and try things and then perform a restoration to a previous state very quickly.

Not every provider will make snapshotting possible for you. In case the system does not support it, then it will give out an error. There are more subcommands which can be used for the purpose of exposing this command. These include the following:

- Push
- Pop
- Delete
- List
- Save
- restore

Snapshot Push

This command takes the syntax given below:

vagrant snapshot push

This command will take a snapshot and then push it back into a snapshot stack. It provides you with a shorthand for "vagrant snapshot save" when you are not in need of specifying a name. Once you have called the inverse of "vagrant snapshot pop," the pushed state will be restored.

Snapshot Pop

The command is used with the syntax given below:

vagrant snapshot pop

It represents the inverse of the command "vagrant snapshot push." It works to restore the state which has been pushed.

Snapshot Save

The command is used with the syntax given below:

vagrant snapshot save NAME

It will name a new snapshot with a name. Once you have used this command, it is not safe for you to use the *"pop"* and *"push"* commands.

Snapshot Restore

This command is used with the following command:

vagrant snapshot restore NAME

The command is used for restoring the snapshot which you specify.

Snapshot List

The command is used with the following syntax:

vagrant snapshot list

Snapshot Delete

The command is used with the following syntax:

vagrant snapshot delete NAME

The command is used for deleting the snapshot which is specified. With some providers, it is required that the child snapshots be deleted. Note that the Vagrant will not track what the children are. This is why you have to delete the snapshots in a reverse order in such a case.

In case the machine is halted in the event of snapshotting, then this command runs faster. In case this is not an option or it is not ideal, then one can use online providers so as to perform the deletion.

Plugin

The command takes the syntax given below:

vagrant plugin

The command is used for the purpose of management of plugins. Subcommands in another sub level are used for the purpose of exposing the functionality of this command. These include the following:

- install
- license
- list
- uninstall
- update

Plugin Install

This command is used with the following syntax:

vagrant plugin install <name>...

The command will install a plugin using the given file path or name. If the specified name does not provide a path to a file, then the plugin will be installed from remote repositories, which is usually the RubyGems. If the plugin is found to have already been installed, then it will be updated, but one can also use the command "vagrant plugin update" for that purpose.

If you specify multiple names, then multiple plugins will be specified. If the flags are given below, the flags will be applied to all the plugins which are being installed by the current command invocation. If the plugin has already been installed, it will be reinstalled using the latest version which is available.

The command will accept only the optional command-line flags:

1. —entry-point ENTRYPOINT- by default, the plugins which have been installed will be loaded internally by use of an initialization file having the same name as the plugin. This is correct most of the time. If the plugin being installed hasanother entrypoint, the flag can be used for the purpose of specifying it.

2. —plugin-cleansources- this will clear all of the sources which have been defined so far. This can be seen to be an advanced feature. It is used for implementing firewalls which prevent access from the RubyGems.org.

3. —plugin-source SOURCE- this is used for adding a source from which the plugin will be added. Note that

with this, the single plugin being installed will not be the one affected, but all of your future plugins. This is a limitation associated with the plugin installer used in Vagrant.

4. —plug-version VERSION- this specifies the version of the plugin which is to be installed, but with the command, the latest version of the plugin will be installed. Note that you can use the flag so as to specify the version of the plug in which you need to install. One can choose to specify the version, or may be use a constraint for the plugin so as to implement a restriction. If you are using various constraints, then use a comma to separate them.

Plugin License

This command takes the syntax given below:

vagrant plugin license <name> <license-file>

It is used for installation of a plugin license for a commercial plugin.

Plugin List

The command takes the following syntax:

vagrant plugin list

The command will list all the plugins which have been installed together with their respective versions. In case you had specified a constraint when installing any plugin, then it will also be listed. Depending on your settings, other information regarding your plugin may also be shown.

Plugin Uninstall

This command takes the following syntax:

vagrant plugin uninstall <name> [<name2> <name3> ...]

The command will uninstall the plugin whose name has been specified. If the plugin has some dependencies and they are not needed by any other plugin, then they will also be uninstalled. Note that it is possible for you to specify multiple plugins, and all of them will be uninstalled.

Plugin Update

This command will take the syntax given below:

vagrant plugin update [<name>]

When the command is used, all the plugins which have been installed with the Vagrant will be updated. Note that the command is good in respecting constraints in case you specified some during installation of the plugin. If you had specified a constraint about the version of the plugin and you need to change this, then use the command "vagrant plugin install" to uninstall it.

If you specify a name, then only that plugin will be updated. However, some people may also specify a plugin which has not been installed. In case this happens, then the command will not install the plugin as some of you might think.

Chapter 5- Vagrant and PHP

One can use a tool named *"Xdebug"* for the purpose of debugging the PHP which is running on your Vagrant. This is done by use of the Host IDE.

With Xdebug, one is allowed to place breakpoints in their PHP code, and then step through your code, allowing you to observe how the variables have been set.

We will edit the grant provision file so that it can automatically install and configure the Xdebug. We will also set up the sublime text so that it can work with the installed Xdbug on Vagrant. We will then install an extension of Chrome, which will make it easier for us to work with the Vagrant.

Installing Xdebug with Vagrant

For us to be able to install Xdebug in Vagrant, we have to begin by installing PEAR, which stands for "**P**HP **E**xtension and **A**pplication **R**epository."

Besides this, we will also install the package PHP5-dev, as this will allow us to install modules to the PHP, and the package "_build-essential_" which allows us to run the commands required for the purpose of building the Xdebug package.

These should be added in the provisioning file so that later, we can add them into the Vagrant. The following command can be used for this purpose:

sudo apt-get -y install mysql-server-5.5 php5-mysql apache2 php5 php5-dev php-pear build-essential

We can then install Xdebug using the command "pecl install xdebug." The command *"pecl"* was installed during the process of installation of PEAR. We also need a place in which we will install our Xdebug logs, The following block of code can be used for creation of this:

mkdir /var/log/xdebug

chown www-data:www-data /var/log/xdebug

sudo pecl install xdebug

The above code will create a directory named *"xdebug"* in the foler "/var/log/." The ownership of the folder is then changed so that the Apche can be in a position to write to it.

Configuration of the PHP

It is now time for us to configure the PHP so that it can be in a position to use Xdebug. This should be done in the file "*php.ini.*" This is shown in the code given below:

```
;;;;;;;;;;;;;;;;;;;;;;;;;

; Added to enable Xdebug ;

;;;;;;;;;;;;;;;;;;;;;;;;;

zend_extension="[enter path here]"

xdebug.default_enable = 1

xdebug.idekey = "vagrant"

xdebug.remote_enable = 1

xdebug.remote_autostart = 0

xdebug.remote_port = 9000
```

xdebug.remote_handler=dbgp

xdebug.remote_log="/var/log/xdebug/xdebug.log"

xdebug.remote_host=10.0.2.2 ; IDE-Environments IP, from vagrant box.

We can then automate how the file *"php.ini"* has been configured. We want to leave this work to Vagrant so that it can do it on our behalf. The following code can be used for this purpose:

```
echo " &gt;&gt; /etc/php5/apache2/php.ini

echo ';;;;;;;;;;;;;;;;;;;;;;;;;;;' &gt;&gt;
/etc/php5/apache2/php.ini

echo '; Added to enable Xdebug ;' &gt;&gt;
/etc/php5/apache2/php.ini
echo ';;;;;;;;;;;;;;;;;;;;;;;;;;;' &gt;&gt;
/etc/php5/apache2/php.ini

echo " &gt;&gt; /etc/php5/apache2/php.ini
```

```
echo 'zend_extension="'$(find / -name 'xdebug.so'
2> /dev/null)'"' >>
/etc/php5/apache2/php.ini

echo 'xdebug.default_enable = 1' >>
/etc/php5/apache2/php.ini

echo 'xdebug.idekey = "vagrant"' >>
/etc/php5/apache2/php.ini

echo 'xdebug.remote_enable = 1' >>
/etc/php5/apache2/php.ini

echo 'xdebug.remote_autostart = 0' >>
/etc/php5/apache2/php.ini

echo 'xdebug.remote_port = 9000' >>
/etc/php5/apache2/php.ini

echo 'xdebug.remote_handler=dbgp' >>
/etc/php5/apache2/php.ini

echo
'xdebug.remote_log="/var/log/xdebug/xdebug.log"'
>> /etc/php5/apache2/php.ini

echo        'xdebug.remote_host=10.0.2.2      ;      IDE-
Environments  IP,  from  vagrant  box.'  >>
/etc/php5/apache2/php.ini
```

With the above block of code, we will do exactly what was

needed in the file *"php.ini."*

The final file for installing the Xdebug and configuring the file

"*php.ini*" should be as shown below:

sudo debconf-set-selections <<< 'mysql-server-5.5 mysql-server/root_password password mypass'

sudo debconf-set-selections <<< 'mysql-server-5.5 mysql-server/root_password_again password mypass' sudo apt-get update sudo apt-get -y install mysql-server-5.5 php5-mysql apache2 php5 php5-dev php-pear build-essential mkdir /var/log/xdebug chown www-data:www-data /var/log/xdebug sudo pecl install xdebug if [! -h /var/www]; then   echo " >> /etc/php5/apache2/php.ini

  echo ';;;;;;;;;;;;;;;;;;;;;;;;;;' >> /etc/php5/apache2/php.ini

  echo '; Added to enable Xdebug ;' >> /etc/php5/apache2/php.ini

  echo ';;;;;;;;;;;;;;;;;;;;;;;;;;' >> /etc/php5/apache2/php.ini

  echo " >> /etc/php5/apache2/php.ini

  echo 'zend_extension="'$(find / -name 'xdebug.so' 2> /dev/null)'"' >> /etc/php5/apache2/php.ini

  echo 'xdebug.default_enable = 1' >> /etc/php5/apache2/php.ini

```
echo 'xdebug.idekey = "vagrant"' >>
/etc/php5/apache2/php.ini

echo 'xdebug.remote_enable = 1' >>
/etc/php5/apache2/php.ini

echo 'xdebug.remote_autostart = 0' >>
/etc/php5/apache2/php.ini

echo 'xdebug.remote_port = 9000' >>
/etc/php5/apache2/php.ini

echo 'xdebug.remote_handler=dbgp' >>
/etc/php5/apache2/php.ini

echo
'xdebug.remote_log="/var/log/xdebug/xdebug.log"'
>> /etc/php5/apache2/php.ini

echo 'xdebug.remote_host=10.0.2.2 ; IDE-
Environments IP, from vagrant box.' >>
/etc/php5/apache2/php.ini


mkdir /vagrant/public

rm -rf /var/www

ln -s /vagrant/public /var/www

a2enmod rewrite

sed -i '/AllowOverride None/c AllowOverride All'
/etc/apache2/sites-available/default

service apache2 restart
```

```
fi


if [ ! -d /vagrant/public/wp-admin ];

then

    cd /vagrant/public

    wget http://wordpress.org/latest.tar.gz

    tar xvf latest.tar.gz

    mv wordpress/* ./

    rmdir ./wordpress/

    rm -f latest.tar.gz

fi


if [ ! -f /var/log/databasesetup ];

then
```

```
mysql -u root -pmypass -e "CREATE DATABASE

wordpress;"

mysql -u root -pmypass -e "CREATE USER
'user1'@'localhost' IDENTIFIED BY 'mypassword';"

mysql -u root -pmypass -e "GRANT ALL
PRIVILEGES ON wordpress.* TO 'user1'@'localhost';"

mysql -u root -pmypass -e "FLUSH PRIVILEGES;"

touch /var/log/databasesetup

fi
```

Now that you have done that, you can navigate to the project's

root and then issue the command given below:

vagrant up

The above command will get everything up and running.

Configuration of Sublime Text for Using Xdebug

If you don't use the sublime text editor in your computer, just use the handy installer to install it.

In this text editor, commands are executed using the key combination of "shift + cmd + p." After that, a prompt box is presented to you, and once you have started typing your commands, all the commands which one can take in advance will be shown.

Once you are done with the above, you can go ahead to install the Xdebug client for your sublime text by pressing the key combination "shift + cmd + p" and then beginning to type _"install."_

After that, just press the *"enter"* key and another prompt will be presented to you. On this prompt, begin to type *"xdebug"* and the following screen will be presented to you:

You can then hit the *"enter"* key, and that will install the Xdebug client for your sublime text.

At this point, our context menu should have a new addition. The Tools menu should now have the option *"Xdebug."*

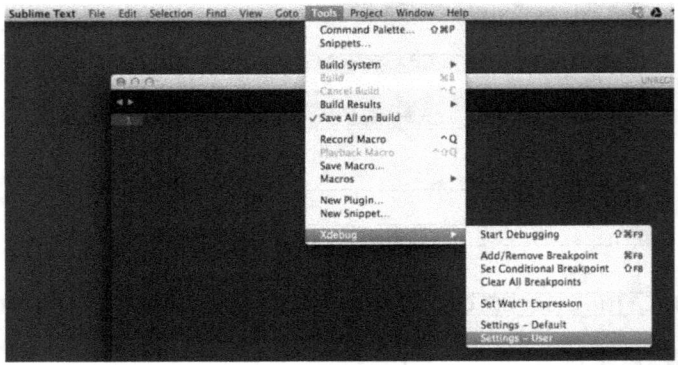

Configuration of the Xdebug Client

Our next step should be to ensure that the Xdebug client has been correctly configured. There are multiple ways that this can be done, but since we are going to have many instances of Vagrant running, it will be good for us if we do it on the basis of a per-project.

We can use the Sublime text editor to create a new project by use of the contextual menu. This can be done by navigating through *"Project > Add Folder to Project..."*

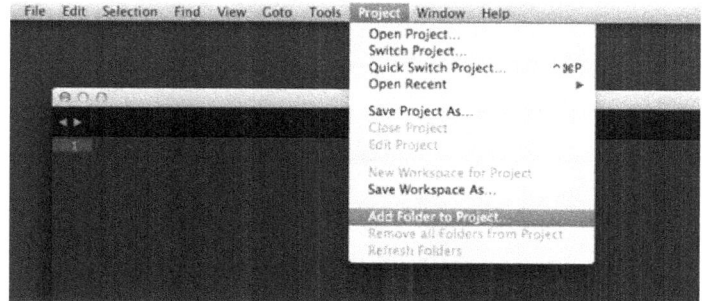

Once you have completed doing all the above, the Sublime text window will provide you with a sidebar which will specify a number of details for your project. Note that the project has not yet been saved. To do this, navigate to *"Project > Save Project As..."* and then save it at the root folder of your project.

Identify the project with the extension ".sublime.project," and then open it up. The file should have some code as shown below:

{

```
"folders":

[

    {

        "follow_symlinks": true,

        "path": "."

    }

]

}
```

Add the following piece of code into the file:

```
"settings": {

    "xdebug": {

        "path_mapping": {
```

```
        "/vagrant/public" : "/Users/[ user name]/[path
to the project]/public",
    },

    "url": "http://localhost:8080/",

    "super_globals": true,

    "close_on_stop": true

  }

}
```

Note that you have to specify the username and the path which leads to the project as specified in the code.

If you put it together, you will have something which looks as follows:

```
{

    "folders":
```

```json
[
    {
        "follow_symlinks": true,

            "path": "."
    }
],
  "settings": {
    "xdebug": {
        "path_mapping": {

            "/vagrant/public" : "/Users/johnjoel/dev/vagrant-wp-base/public",

        },

      "url": "http://localhost:8080/",

      "super_globals": true,

      "close_on_stop": true
```

```
        }

    }

}
```

You can save the file and then open it up using the sublime text. The project should launch.

Testing

You can at this point perform your testing. Launch your browser, then open the URL "**http://localhost:8080**" and this will present you with the start page of your WordPress installer.

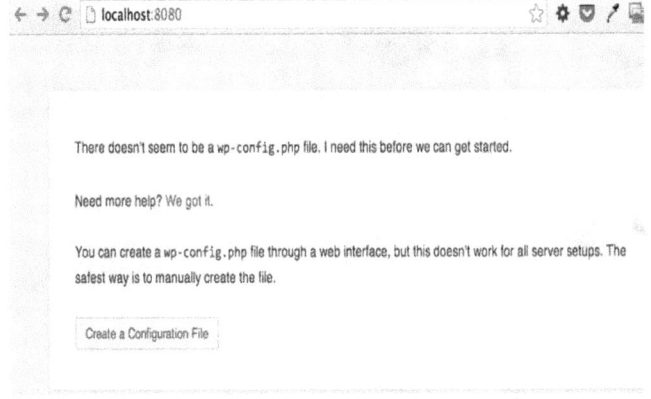

Nothing should happen at this point, as there still two things which we have not done:

1. Starting of debugging

2. Addition of breakpoint to the project

In the Sublime text, navigate to the directory "/public/index.php" and then to the first big of the PHP code you find on the page. Right click and open the context menu which will allow you to add a breakpoint to the page.

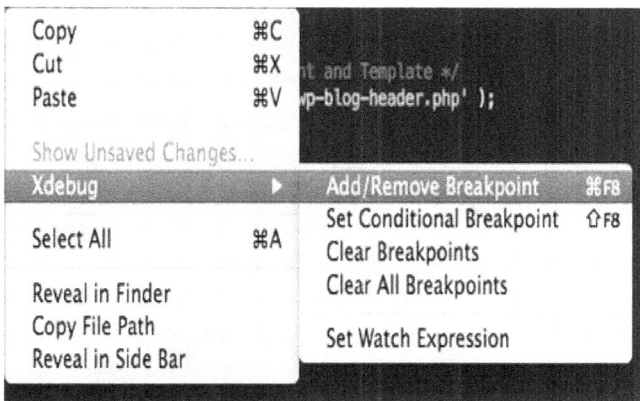

The above should add a breakpoint to your code. We can then fire up our debugger by hitting *"Tools > Xdebug > Start Debugging"* or by hitting "command + F9." New panels will be presented in the Sublime text, and these will present you with the debug information. The Xdebug Breakpoint window will provide you with the information regarding the breakpoint which we recently inserted.

Chapter 6- Facts, Conditionals and Modules

We are going to explore how these can be used in Vagrant and puppet.

Facts

Facts can be seen as being the same as variables, with the exception being that they have been predefined. In puppet, a tool named *"Facter"* is used for the purpose of collecting information about the system we are using. Facts are used for representation of the data that is obtained.

Facts are used widely in puppet modules which are open source, and they make these very versatile.

Custom Facts

These are created by users for the purpose of providing extra information to puppet. Sometimes, you may need to write facts which are specific to a particular site data, which is not only available via Facter, but we are in need of including it in a template. Consider the example given below, which shows how shell commands can be used in facts:

```
# hardware_platform.rb
Facter.add('hardware_platform') do
 setcode do
   Facter::Core::Execution.exec('/bin/uname --hardware-platform')
 end
end
```

Using Other Facts

To write a fact which uses other facts, we can use *"Facter.value(:afact)"*. In case the fact has failed to resolve, or is not found, the Facter will return nil. Consider the example given below:

```
Facter.add(:osfamily) do
 setcode do
  distid = Facter.value(:lsbdistid)
  case distid
  when /RedHatEnterprise|CentOS|Fedora/
   'redhat'
  when 'ubuntu'
   'debian'
  else
   distid
  end
 end
end
```

end

Configuration of Facts

The *"confine"* statement is very common when it comes to use of Facts in Vagrant. This is used for restricting a Fact to be executable only when a system which has a specified and similar fact.

Consider the example given below, which shows how the *"confine"* statement can be used:

```
Facter.add(:powerstates) do
 confine :kernel => 'Linux'
 setcode do
   Facter::Core::Execution.exec('cat
/sys/power/states')
 end
```

end

The above fact will make use of sysfs in Linux so as to get the list of power states available on a particular system. Note that this can only be run on Linux.

Fact Precedence

A single fact can have multiple resolutions, and each of these try to ascertain what we should take the value of the fact to be. The weight of a fact is defined by the number of confines for that specific resolution. Consider the example given below which best demonstrates this:

 # Checking to be sure that this server has been marked as the postgres #server

Facter.add(:role) do

 has_weight 100

```
  setcode do

    if File.exist? '/etc/postgres_server'

      'postgres_server'

    end

  end

end


# Guessing if it is a server by presence of pg_create
binary

Facter.add(:role) do

  has_weight 50

  setcode do

    if File.exist? '/usr/sbin/pg_create'

      'postgres_server'

    end

  end

end


# If the server does not look like a server, it should be
a desktop

Facter.add(:role) do
```

```
setcode do

  'desktop'

 end

end
```

Execution Timeouts

Timeouts should be passed to "Facter::Core::Execution#execute." This is shown in the code given below:

```
Facter.add(:sleep) do

 setcode do

  begin

    Facter::Core::Execution.execute('sleep          10',
:timeout => 5)

    'failed to timeout!'

  rescue Facter::Core::Execution::ExecutionFailure

    'timeout!'
```

end

   end

end

Aggregate Resolutions

In case your fact is combining multiple commands, then it will be good for you to use _"aggregate resolutions."_ There is a great difference between aggregate resolutions and simple resolutions. For an aggregate resolution to be used, one has to introduce the parameter ":type => :aggregate." This is shown below:

```
Facter.add(:fact_name, :type => :aggregate) do
   #chunks should be added here
   #aggregate block should be added here
End
```

Each step in your resolution will get its own chunck with a name as shown below:

chunk(:one) do

  'Chunk one should return this. '

end

chunk(:two) do

  'Chunk two should return this.'

end

For the case of simple resolutions, one has to use the statement "setcode" which will be used for setting the value of the fact. However, this statement is never used in aggregate resolutions. These have an aggregate block used for the task of combination of chunks. This is what returns the value of your fact.

Consider the example given below used for combination of two chunks:

```ruby
aggregate do |chunks|

  result = ''

  chunks.each_value do |str|

    result += str

  end


  # The sesult will be "Chunk one should return this.
  Chunk two should return this."

  result

end
```

External Facts in Unix

In Unix, external facts will work by dropping an executable file into a standard external fact path. One always needs a shebang for execution of external facts in Unix. If the shebang is not specified, then the script will not be executed, but it will fail.

Consider the example of external fact given below:

```
#!/usr/bin/env python
data = {"key1" : "val1", "key2" : "val2" }

for j in data:
   print "%s=%s" % (j,data[j])
```

The above is an external fact in Python programming language.

To check if you have set the execute bit of the script, use the command given below:

chmod +x /etc/facter/facts.d/my_fact_script.py

For the Facter to parse your output, the script has to return key/value pairs in the format given below on the STDOUT:

key1=val1

key2=val2

key3=val3

When we use the format given above, then a single script will return multiple facts.

Conditionals

Puppet provides us with condition statements just like any other programming language you can think of. The *"if"* statement in puppet can be used as shown below:

```
if $operatingsystem == 'Ubuntu' {

 notice('Cool! I really enjoy using Ubuntu ')

}
elsif $operatingsystem == 'Windows' {

 warning('What are you really doing...')

}
else {

 notice("I am not aware of what you think about ${operatingsystem}. It belongs to ${osfamily}, isnt it?")

}
```

Note the facts which have been used in the above example and they include "$operatingsystem" and "osfamily." The above piece of code can be added to the default.pp and then execute the *"vagrant provision."*

Modules

The Puppet Modules will give you the ability to split the puppet config into components which are functional, separated, and reusable. You should create a module which will be used for holding the puppet modules. Inside your *"puppet"* folder, create a new folder, and then give it the name *"modules."* The modules path has to be defined inside the Vagrantfile, by adding the line given below to the puppet block:

puppet.module_path = "puppet/modules"

The puppet will then have to look for the modules inside the path *"puppet/modules."*

Creating Modules

The following are some of the guidelines for modules:

1. The module has to go in a directory, and the name of this directory should be the name of your module.

2. The directory must have a *"manifests"* sub-directory for holding files with a .pp extension.

3. The manifest has to be named init.pp, and then hold a single class definition. This should have the same name as your module.

At this point, we can turn the default.pp so that it can have two modules, that is, apache and system-update. It should have a structure similar to the one given below:

- **Project Root (./)**

- **puppet**
  - **manifests**
    - **default.pp**
  - **modules**
    - **apache**
      - **manifests**
        - **init.pp**
    - **system-update**
      - **manifests**
        - **init.pp**
- **Vagrantfile**
- **(...)**

The above structure may look to be a bit complex compared to the old default.pp file, but this is very important in real life since in most cases, much is expected from server computers. When we define all the configuration in a single default.pp file, the maintenance and configuration will be a bit confusing. Puppet can be thought as being another programming language and the more it gets modular, the more it becomes reusable in the future, and the process of adding and removing modules is made much easier.

We can then copy the classes to the new module file named *"init,pp"* as shown below:

```
class apache {
 package { "apache2":
  ensure => present,
  require => Class["system-update"],
}
 service { "apache2":
  ensure => "running",
  require => Package["apache2"],
}
}
```

The above code should be followed with the following code:

```
class system-update {
```

```
exec { 'apt-get update':

  command => 'apt-get update',

}

$sysPackages = [ "build-essential" ]

package { $sysPackages:

  ensure => "installed",

  require => Exec['apt-get update'],

}

}
```

The file default.pp should now be as shown below:

```
Exec { path => [ "/bin/", "/sbin/" , "/usr/bin/",
"/usr/sbin/" ] }

include apache

include system-update
```

At this point, feel free to run the provision, and you will observe that you get the same result as previously, with the only exception being that you have your configurations being split into components which are reusable.

You are now aware of basic classes and even how to use basic facts in them. Sometimes, we might need to use real parameters inside them, just as we do in object-oriented programming.

This can be done similarly as it is done in PHP as shown below:

```
class apache( $document_root = '/var/www', $port = 80)
{
  #The code for the class
}
```

You must have learned before that the module classes can be included and we have no place for the parameters in the include and our classes can be called in another way and then some parameters passed along. Classes which are dependent on parameters can be implemented in such a way as shown below:

```
class { "apache":
 "documentroot" => "/vagrant"
}
```

For our modules to be added as sub-modules of Git, use the command given below:

git submodule add [repository-url] [final folder]

The following command can be used for the purpose of addition of the module for Apache:

```
$ git submodule add
https://github.com/example1/puppet-apache.git
puppet/modules/apache
```

Note that the above command should be run from your root Git folder. The name of the directory and that of the main module class must have the same name. The file default.pp should now be as follows:

```
Exec { path => [ "/bin/", "/sbin/" , "/usr/bin/",
"/usr/sbin/" ] }
exec { 'apt-get update':
 command => 'apt-get update',
 timeout => 60,
 tries   => 3
}


class { 'apt':
 always_apt_update => true,
}


package { ['python-software-properties']:
 ensure  => 'installed',
 require => Exec['apt-get update'],
```

```
}


$sysPackages = [ 'build-essential', 'git', 'curl']

package { $sysPackages:

 ensure => "installed",

 require => Exec['apt-get update'],

}

class { "apache": }


apache::module { 'rewrite': }


apache::vhost { 'default':

 docroot          => '/vagrant/web',

 server_name      => false,

 priority         => ",

 template         =>

'apache/virtualhost/vhost.conf.erb',

}


apt::ppa { 'ppa:ondrej/php5':
```

```
  before  => Class['php'],

}


class { 'php': }


$phpModules = [ 'imagick', 'xdebug', 'curl', 'mysql',
'cli', 'intl', 'mcrypt', 'memcache']

php::module { $phpModules: }


php::ini { 'php':

 value   => ['date.timezone = "USA/New York"'],

 target  => 'php.ini',

 service => 'apache',

}
```

Conclusion

We have come to the conclusion of this guide. Vagrant lets its users create reproducible, lightweight, and portable development environments. When you compare this tool with other tools such as KVM, Virtualization, and VMWare, this tool can be seen as a high-level wrapper. The original version of Vagrant had been tied up to the Virtyualbox, but with the late releases, other software such as VMWare and KVM are supported.

Note that Vagrant was written in the Ruby programming language. However, it doesn't mean that it can only run on such environments as projects written in programming languages such as Java, PHP, and Python can also run on it. The Vagrant tool has also been improved so that it can be in a position to support Docker containers. The containers can be used as a substitute or alternative for a full operating system.

Vagrant has several plug-INS which its users can take advantage of so as to perform extra functionalities.

The good thing with Vagrant is that it is a versatile tool. One can run it on Windows, Mac OS X, or any popular Linux distribution. My hope is that this guide has helped you learn some of the uses of Vagrant. Enjoy!

www.ingramcontent.com/pod-product-compliance
Lightning Source LLC
Chambersburg PA
CBHW060947050326
40689CB00012B/2579